MERL

JOHN & CAITLÍN MATTHEWS

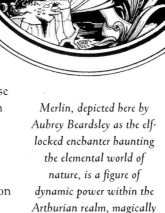

Merlin has been portrayed in many different ways throughout the ages. The oldest references, in Celtic myth and story, describe him as a shaman, bard, seer and prophet, but it is the medieval stories that have made him a household name. In these he is seen as a wizard and wise man, and as a powerful influence in the stories of King Arthur and his knights. The Celtic sources are important because the story of Merlin in its purest form draws entirely upon native British tradition and belief, while the Arthurian legends show the influence of French and Germanic story-tellers.

Merlin's greatest vision was of the Round Table, where all men would meet as equals. In time, however, this image of a perfect society was to be broken by the internecine quarrels of the knights, the illicit love of Lancelot and Guinevere, and by the bitterness of Arthur's own son,

Merlin, depicted here by Aubrey Beardsley as the elf-locked enchanter haunting the elemental world of nature, is a figure of dynamic power within the Arthurian realm, magically overseeing affairs of state.

Mordred. It is small wonder that Merlin chose to flee from the world of men to a celestial observatory where he lived out the rest of his days in the study of the starry heavens – a far more productive study than that of human frailty.

In our own time, many books, plays and films have been devoted to Merlin, who has re-emerged as guide or mentor in a variety of new guises, such as the characters of Obi-Wan Kenobi in George Lucas's *Star Wars* trilogy and Gandalf in J.R.R. Tolkien's *Lord of the Rings*.

Despite all the years which have elapsed since Merlin first appeared in literature and tradition, his personality has changed very little. He is still, to this day, regarded widely as a wise and beneficent being, whose actions and purpose, while seldom wholly revealed, suggest an ongoing, mysterious influence in the affairs of the human race.

THE MANY FACES OF MERLIN

Gustave Doré's oak-crowned, druidic Merlin, pictured here with an adoring Vivienne (Nimue), shows the venerable yet fallible face of the sage.

Merlin appears as an other-worldly alien to men, instilling superstitious fear, yet, to the youthful King Arthur, he is an insightful counsellor, guiding him through all the perils of kingship.

When we think of Merlin we tend to imagine a single person, but there are several Merlin figures deriving from a shadowy character dating back to an ancient tradition of oral storytelling. The first Merlin was probably a shaman: a tribal visionary and healer who cared for both the physical and spiritual well-being of his people.

The oldest figure of whom we have any real knowledge is *Myrddin Wyllt* (Merlin the Wild, or Merlin the Mad). Even so, we still know very little about him apart from a few brief references in early Celtic texts and a scattering of poems attributed to him. In one of these poems he describes his existence as an outcast, living wild in the woods. The poem is addressed to a pet pig who shares his rough life and to whom he utters various prophecies. Pigs were regarded as sacred by the Celts and there are references to several such oracular beasts in the literature of the time. Myrddin Wyllt is associated with northern Britain.

Another figure, called *Myrddin Emrys* (or *Merlin Ambrosius* in the Latin form), more closely resembles the Merlin we know today. He is largely the invention of the 12th-century writer Geoffrey of Monmouth, who included the story of Merlin in his *Historiae Regum Britanniae* (*History of the Kings of Britain*), which draws largely upon early chroniclers and Celtic myth. In this, Geoffrey paints a dramatic picture of Merlin as a wise child who grows up to become the chief counsellor to the young King Arthur, dynastically shaping the rulers of Britain.

These three aspects of Merlin have continued to influence writers ever since. In our own time, John Cowper Powys, in *Porius*, portrays Merlin as a shamanic figure, while in cycles of books such as Mary Stewart's trilogy of novels, which begins with the *Crystal Cave*, Bernard Cornwell's *Warlord Chronicles* and Susan Cooper's *Dark Is Rising* sequence, the authors combine the medieval and the Celtic in their portraits of the wizard.

Obi-Wan Kenobi, the mystical Jedi knight in George Lucas's Star Wars trilogy draws much of his character and significance from the more familiar character of Merlin. Both have remarkable powers and both act as counsellors to young heroes.

THE COMING OF MERLIN

The tale related in
Geoffrey of Monmouth's *History* is a
timeless myth, pre-dating the more familiar
stories of Merlin. It tells how the usurping King
Vortigern sought to build a castle for himself in the mountain-
ous region of Snowdonia but, every time the walls reached a certain
height, they fell down. No one could explain this, but Vortigern's druids
suggested that the only solution was to water the stones with the blood of a
child who had no father. Soldiers were sent by Vortigern to seek this wondrous
child and, as they passed through the town of Carmarthen, they overheard two
boys fighting. One was taunting the other as being 'fatherless' and the soldiers
discovered that the boy, whose name was Emrys (Ambrosius), was the son of a local
princess, although his father was believed to be one of the Faery race.
The soldiers took the child to Vortigern, who prepared to sacrifice him. However, the boy
revealed that the castle could not be built because of the presence of two dragons, who
fought every night beneath the hill, and whose battle caused the walls to tumble. Vortigern
ordered the site to be excavated, and the dragons burst forth and fought each other in the
skies above the hill. It was at this point that the boy uttered a series of prophecies. Fear of
the power thus displayed not only caused Vortigern to spare the boy's life but established
the young Emrys (later known as Merlin) as the foremost prophet of his time.
The hill where these events were believed to have
occurred became known as *Dinas Emrys* (Fort of Emrys)
and the ruins of Vortigern's castle can still
be seen there to this day. The child grew
into a man and became an instrument in the
fate that brought another wondrous youth,
Arthur, to the throne of Britain.

*Merlin, shown here as a
tiny baby, in an image
reminiscent of the Virgin
and Child, is the son of a
Welsh princess and an
other-worldly spirit. Half
mortal and half immortal,
he has a unique insight into
human and spiritual events.*

*Merlin's mother is depicted here with an
other-worldly lover in the act of conceiving
Merlin. Thus he is chosen to be the sacrifice
by Vortigern's magicians, who assert that only
the blood of a fatherless boy can cement the
foundations of the falling tower.*

Most early sources represent Merlin with natural psychic gifts, but later texts give Merlin a wise mentor in the shape of Master Blaise, who lives alone in the woods of Northumberland and is held by some to be even wiser than his pupil.

The dragons that demolish the usurping King Vortigern's tower are uncovered by the boy, Emrys, who prophesies a long combat between Britain (represented by the red dragon) and her enemies (represented by the white dragon).

MERLIN THE WILD

Right: *The earliest Welsh texts tell of Merlin as Myrrdin Wyllt, or Merlin the Wild, driven mad by terrible sights of slaughter. In this etching by Alan Lee, Merlin is shown hiding in the vast Caledonian Forest, almost at one with the trees.*

The three deaths which Merlin prophesies for the youth brought to him by Ganeida are depicted here. This triple death motif is the remnant of a sacrificial ritual practised in early north-western Europe.

Geoffrey of Monmouth also wrote *Vita Merlini* (*Life of Merlin*) in which he related the story of Merlin the Wild. In this we learn that Merlin was driven mad by events in the battle of Arfderydd, in which his three brothers were killed. As a result he fled to the Caledonian forest where he lived off the land as a wildman, making 'perpetual lamentation'.

Of the many attempts to restore Merlin to his right mind, only the poet Taliesin was successful, drawing him out by intricate discussions of the nature of weather and the creation of the world. Efforts were also made to discredit his prophetic powers; his sister Ganeida brought the same youth, wearing different costumes, to Merlin three times so that he might be deceived. Merlin prophesied three different deaths for the youth: that he would fall from a rock, hang from a tree and drown. All three came true, for the youth fell from a high cliff and became caught in a tree, from which he was suspended with his head beneath the water.

Geoffrey of Monmouth was almost certainly trying to reconcile his own version of the story with traditions concerning an older, shamanic figure. He thus gives us a more primitive account of the wild and prophetic seer of the north than in his previous book.

Prophecies and tales surrounding Merlin's own death closely mimic those of a legendary Celtic prophet called Lailoken, who prophesied his own triple death. This theme relates directly to a ritualised form of sacrifice which was practised from earliest times by the peoples of north-western Europe. A body discovered in a Cheshire peat-bog in 1984, and several bodies found in Denmark, suffered a similar death by stabbing, strangulation and drowning, which suggests the appeasement of the powers of earth, air and water.

Merlin is thus seen as owing much to the tradition of the Wild Man, whom medieval writers considered as a 'natural man', poised between the states of wildness and civilisation, and belonging to a lost golden age.

This is especially poignant when we consider that Merlin himself strove to re-create that golden time, a perfect earthly kingdom over which Arthur, his protégé, would come to rule.

Lindow Man, found in a Cheshire peat-bog in 1984 and now in the British Museum, is a graphic example of the three-fold death, as prophesied by Merlin in Geoffrey of Monmouth's Life of Merlin. This man had been stabbed, garrotted and finally drowned.

MERLIN AND KING ARTHUR

When King Uther Pendragon desired Igraine, wife of Gorlois, Duke of Cornwall, Merlin magically disguised Uther to appear like Gorlois and thus Arthur was conceived.

Merlin instigates the test of the Sword in the Stone to reveal the unknown boy, Arthur, as the true son of King Uther. Although many attempted to draw forth the sword, only Arthur was successful.

Merlin acted as King Arthur's mentor and counsellor throughout the best part of his reign until imprisoned by Nimue. Here, knowing his fate, Merlin bids farewell to his protégé for the last time.

Merlin's association with King Arthur, Britain's great hero, is an enduring one. The earliest surviving references to the seer feature him prophesying the coming of the new king, who will sweep away all that went before and reunite the fragmented kingdom of Britain. He later arranges the birth of Arthur by assisting King Uther Pendragon when he falls in love with Igraine, the wife of his former ally, Gorlois of Cornwall. With his magic, Merlin disguises Uther to look like Gorlois so that Igraine will admit the king to her bed. The resulting child is Arthur, whose birth is legitimised by the timely death of Igraine's husband and her subsequent marriage to Uther.

Merlin's dynastic plans are thus brought to fulfilment, and Arthur is crowned king of Britain after he draws the Sword from the Stone. This event is also organised by Merlin, who places the magical weapon, with its legend 'Whoso pulleth out this sword of this stone is rightwise king born of all England', where Arthur will find it and sees to it that he alone can free it from its rocky sheath. Later, when this sword breaks, it is Merlin again who leads Arthur to the Lady of the Lake and persuades her to give him the magical sword, Excalibur.

Merlin's continued presence shapes the destiny of the young king; he helps Arthur to win battles, advises him at every step of the way, enables him to build the great city of Camelot and warns him against the evil machinations of his half-sisters, Morgan le Fay and Morgause.

It is one of the great tragedies of the Arthurian tradition that, despite his prophetic skills, Merlin is unable to save Arthur from the darker side of his destiny: the love affair between his queen, Guinevere, and his best knight, Lancelot, and the hatred and jealousy of his bastard son, Mordred.

MERLIN AND THE ROUND TABLE

In Sir Thomas
Malory's 15th-century book *Le Morte
d'Arthur* (*The Death of Arthur*), Merlin is credited
with the creation of the Round Table, the symbol of good
government around which King Arthur's reign is firmly established. Merlin's earlier accomplishment of raising the Giant's Dance,
or the Hanging Stones of Stonehenge, related by Geoffrey of Monmouth,
seems to pre-figure this story. There, these stones were magically transferred
from *Killarus* (Kildare) in Ireland and set up on Salisbury Plain as a memorial to
British nobles treacherously slain by the Saxons. The stone circle had actually been
standing for thousands of years before Merlin's time, but this story may well have
suggested the idea of a meeting-place where all were equal.
In the 12th-century poem known as Layamon's *Brut*, the first major work written in English
after the Norman Conquest, we read of a mysterious 'craftsman' who came before Arthur and
offered to build him a circular table which would seat 1,600 people and at which all would be equal.
Although he is unnamed, it is possible to see Merlin as a prototype of this character. In Malory's
Le Morte d'Arthur it is the wizard who orders the table's construction and who says specifically
that he is making it 'round, in the likeness of the world'.
The assemblies of King Arthur's knights are said to have taken place at various places,
notably Caerleon and Carlisle, and Camelot – the legendary court which has been ascribed
to many sites, including Cadbury Castle in Somerset and the Great Hall of Winchester.
These gatherings were notably held at Whitsun (Pentecost), when the worthies of the island
gathered to share news of deeds done or injustices to be righted. The instruments of the
Round Table are King Arthur's knights, who go forth throughout the land to police unrest,
subdue tyrants and protect the weak.
The most notable assembly of all is that which establishes the Grail Quest, although
Merlin has little to do with this. His involvement in Arthur's story occurs primarily
in the earlier half of the king's reign, but he foresees the coming of the Grail
and prepares for its mystical appearance by
emphasising the importance of spiritual
values among the Knights of the
Round Table.

Sir

Sir Sagris.   *Sir* Bors.

*Stonehenge is the forerunner
of the Round Table. A place
of sacred gathering since
prehistory, its magical
building is ascribed to Merlin
by the 12th-century writer
Geoffrey of Monmouth.*

Sir Gauwin.

Sir Ector.

Sir Galahad.

Sir Gareth.

Sir Kay.

Sir Triſtram.

Sir Gaheris.

Sir Beaumans.

Sir Berſunt.

Sir Pe

The Round Table at Winchester Great Hall is a Tudor recreation of King Arthur's own Round Table, at which the chief knights had their names engraved over each siège, or seat. A portrait of Henry VIII, in the guise of Arthur, adorns the head of the board.

Wynkyn de Worde's 16th-century vision of the Round Table shows Arthur seated in the middle, surrounded by his knights. Merlin is said to have created the Round Table in the likeness of the roundness of the globe.

ell. sir Superablilis.

sir Perciuall.

sir Marhaus.

sir Ballamor

sir Acolon.

In John Boorman's film Excalibur, Merlin (Nicol Williamson) galvanises the feuding knights into a unified circle under the Red Dragon banner of King Arthur, so that they are 'one under the stars'.

sir Launcelot.

sir Galohalt.

sir Beleobus-

sir Floll.

sir Paginet.

sir Belvoure.

sir Palamide.

sir Turqnine.

sir Tor.

sir Lamarecke.

MERLIN'S ISLE

The dramatic Dark Age fortress of Dinas Emrys in Snowdonia is the site of the boy Merlin's struggle against Vortigern, the place where the dragons are imprisoned until released by Merlin's prophecies.

This face was carved c.1840 by the stonemason Robert Garner, great-grandfather of Alan Garner, whose celebrated book The Weirdstone of Brisingamen is based on the legend of Alderley Edge.

A pre-12th-century text, *Enweu
Ynys Prydein (Names of the Island of Britain)*,
speaks of Britain as *Clas Myrddin* (Merlin's Precinct),
while in Edmund Spenser's 16th-century *Faerie Queene* Merlin is
credited with building a protective wall of brass around the land. Such
stories indicate the importance of Merlin as a guardian spirit of Britain, and
certainly a number of places throughout the country feature his name.
In Wales, local stories about Dinas Emrys reflect the encounters between Merlin and
Vortigern, while Carmarthen claims that its name is derived from 'Merlin'. An ancient
tree that stood in the centre of Carmarthen was known as Merlin's Oak and tradition
held that, should it be removed, the town would fall.
In Cheshire, according to local legend, Merlin provisioned a cave beneath Alderley Edge
where Arthur and his men still lie sleeping, awaiting their country's need. On a nearby rock
is a carving, believed to represent the face of Merlin, beneath which are the words 'Drink of this
and take thy fill, for the water falls by the wizard's will'.
Recent evidence presented by Nikolai Tolstoy indicates a strong connection between Merlin and
Hart Fell in Dumfriesshire, Scotland. At the head of a precipitous valley there is a small cave to which
Merlin is believed to have fled after the battle of Arfderydd. Near Dumbarton, in the shadow of
Drumelzier (Merlin's Hill) and close by the hamlet of Merlindale, a small cairn of stones marks
the possible last resting place of at least one of the many Merlins.
This grave lies near where the Pewsail enters the River Tweed.
Thomas the Rhymer, a medieval Scottish poet and prophet, foretold:
*When Tweed and Powsail meet at Merlin's grave,
Scotland and England that day a king shall have.*
This prophecy was fulfilled in 1603, when James VI of Scotland was crowned
James I of England, and floodwaters rose and briefly met as the two countries
were united under one king.
Further south, in the market town of Marlborough, Wiltshire, stands a
pyramid-shaped hill known as Merlin's Tump. Although traditionally
associated with Merlin's grave since the 13th century, it is
recorded in the Domesday Book as 'Maerlebri', a name
of Saxon rather than Celtic origin.

*At Hart Fell in Scotland lies the cave where, tradition holds,
Merlin lived after being driven mad by the death of his brothers in
battle. The great Caledonian Forest once covered this area, and
there are several local stories of Merlin's presence there.*

MERLIN'S LAND

She is not any common Earth,
Water or wood or air,
But Merlin's Isle of Gramarye
Where you and I shall fare.

'PUCK'S SONG' BY RUDYARD KIPLING

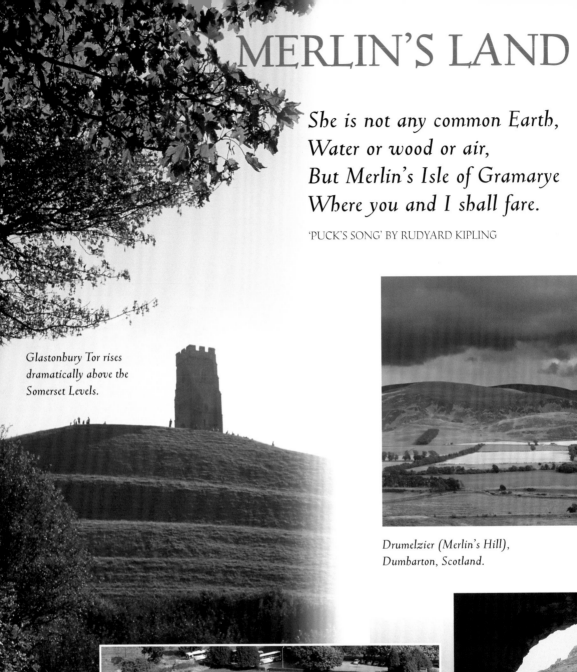

Glastonbury Tor rises dramatically above the Somerset Levels.

Drumelzier (Merlin's Hill), Dumbarton, Scotland.

Circular Roman amphitheatre at Caerleon-on-Usk.

View from Merlin's Cave, Tintagel, Cornwall.

SITES ASSOCIATED WITH MERLIN:

1. Alderley Edge (Merlin's Rock)
2. Arfderydd
3. Bardsey Island (Ynys Enlli)
4. Bath
5. Cadbury Castle
6. Caerleon
7. Carlisle
8. Carmarthen
9. Dinas Emrys (Fort of Emrys)
10. Dozmary Pool
11. Drumelzier (Merlin's Hill)
12. Eildon Hills
13. Glastonbury Tor
14. Hart Fell
15. Marlborough (Merlin's Tump)
16. Merlin's Bridge
17. Merlin's Cave
18. Moat of Liddel/Ardrydd
19. Mynydd Myrddin
20. Myrddin's Quoit
21. Oxford
22. Pendragon Castle
23. Stonehenge
24. Tintagel Castle
25. Winchester

In Malory's Le Morte d'Arthur *(illustrated by Arthur Rackham), Nimue persuades Merlin to enter the cave, where he is imprisoned. After his withdrawal, she herself takes over his prophetic role at Camelot.*

Merlin shows a marked respect for women and is associated with several, notably the Lady of the Lake, who gives the magical sword, Excalibur, to Arthur at Merlin's request. In the medieval texts, Merlin assists Arthur to combat the enchantments of Morgan le Fay and Morgause, the king's half-sisters, who continually seek to overthrow him. Here, as often in later stories, Morgan particularly is seen as a destructive figure but, in the earlier *Life of Merlin*, the poet Taliesin reminds Merlin of how, together, they carried the body of the mortally wounded Arthur to the island of Avalon, to be cared for by Morgen and her eight sisters. Morgen is the Queen of Avalon, an ancient guardian of the land and a figure worthy to receive Arthur and restore him to the realm of Britain once again.

The more ancient Celtic sources speak of Merlin's sister, Gwenddydd, who was reputed to be as skilled a seer as her brother. Merlin expresses guilt at being responsible for the death of her son and daughter, although the details of this story have not survived. The 12th-century *Red Book of Hergest* contains a dialogue between Merlin and Gwenddydd in which she returns prophecy for prophecy. Geoffrey of Monmouth embroiders the relationship further, calling her Ganeida and having her comfort Merlin during his madness. After his cure she builds him an observatory to which he retires, leaving the task of prophecy to Ganeida.

This retirement of Merlin is elaborated in later medieval texts, where the character of Nimue (also called Vivienne) replaces Gwenddydd/Ganeida in a more sinister fashion. In these versions of the story it is Merlin who builds a hidden retreat, protected by magic, for Nimue. Moreover, Merlin is portrayed as a lecherous dotard, stalking Nimue, who takes her revenge by turning his magical powers against him. It seems that the pious medieval writers, being unable to accept the idea of brother and sister sharing a house together, with its implication of incest, turned the story on its head, giving Nimue the magical home in which she imprisons her suitor in enchanted sleep.

This illustration from the 13th-century Douce History of Merlin *shows the bedazzled sage teaching his knowledge to Nimue, little knowing she will turn it upon him.*

*Merlin and Vivien by Sidney Harold Meteyard shows
Merlin as an alchemist in his laboratory. She begs for
initiation into the magical knowledge that will eventually
lead to Merlin's withdrawal from the world.*

*Morgen, queen of the other-
worldly island of Avalon,
depicted here by Stuart
Littlejohn, is the healer of
the mortally wounded King
Arthur in Geoffrey of
Monmouth's* Life of
Merlin. *Later medieval
writers overlaid her beneficent character with witch-
like qualities.*

*When the Sword from the
Stone broke in battle, the
Lady of the Lake gave
King Arthur his magical
sword, Excalibur, at
Merlin's request.*

MERLIN IN THE TIDE OF TIME

Thong Castle.

Merlin's prophecies touch every age and chiefly concern the defence of the realm of Britain, whose spiritual guardian he is held to be in Welsh tradition. In this painting by Richard Hooke, he is shown surrounded by warriors of many ages.

Merlin's prophecies have excited every generation and have been widely interpreted for contemporary relevance. Merlin, shown here in monastic guise at Thong Castle, near Lincoln, reads over his prophecies while heraldic and legendary beasts sport in the landscape.

The red Dragon

Welsh bardic lore speaks of Merlin as the guardian of the Thirteen Treasures of Britain. These were sacred emblems and objects like this ritual cauldron found in Denmark, whose priestly or kingly use maintained the integrity of the realm.

In Geoffrey of Monmouth's *Life of Merlin*, Merlin's sister Ganeida (Gwenddydd) prepares an observatory with 70 doors and windows from which he can keep vigil over the land of Britain. This tradition passes into later legend as Merlin's House of Glass, in which he guards the Thirteen Treasures of Britain, and is a story which is applied to *Ynys Enlli* (Bardsey Island), off the west coast of Wales.

These treasures are the empowering emblems of Britain and, rather than conferring wealth, are more properly understood to be 'hallows', or sacred emblems, by which the realm is governed. Just as the coronation regalia of a monarch are symbolic of more than sovereignty, conferring rights, powers and privileges, so too the Thirteen Treasures embody the enduring powers of 'Merlin's Precinct'.

Among the significant objects included in this collection of Treasures are several that belonged to mythical heroes of old. These include the Cauldron of Dwrnach the Giant, the Whetstone of Tudwal, Arthur's Mantle of Invisibility, together with his knife Carnwennan, the Coat of Padarn Redcoat, the Dish of Rhygenydd and the magical Basket of Gwyddno Garanhir.

Some of these hallowed objects later passed into the accounts of the Grail Quest, which was a journey in search not only of the sacred vessel itself, but also of the Spear, the Sword and the Stone. The fact that Merlin is recognised as the guardian of the Treasures in the oldest versions of his story is a further indication of his importance in the magical history of Britain.

Merlin the prophet has never really gone away. During the 17th century, books of his prophecies were regularly reprinted, vying with each other as a source of insight into both the present and future. In our own time, numerous writers have chosen the figure of Merlin to represent the magical and the mysterious, while a recent book, *The Merlin Mystery*, by Jonathan Gunson and Marten Coombe, instituted a country-wide treasure hunt for 'Merlin's Staff', a modern artefact inspired by this great story of the wizard.

Ynys Enlli (Bardsey Island) is a holy island off the west coast of Wales. It is traditionally the true place of Merlin's retirement from the world, from where he still vigilantly oversees the affairs of Britain.

THE DEPARTURE OF MERLIN

Although Merlin's final rest-
ing place may never be known, in the stories
the mystery of Merlin's departure is more profound.
One such story, the medieval *Didot Percival*, describes the great
prophet retiring to an '*esplumoir*'. The exact meaning of this word
remains uncertain, although it is usually translated as 'moulting cage'. Since
the merlin was one of the favourite hunting-birds in medieval times, perhaps the
writer of the story, or Merlin himself, was making a punning reference to the cages
where such birds were placed to moult and renew their feathers.
According to the medieval French *Estoire de Merlin* (*Story of Merlin*) the last person to
hear the voice of the great magician was the knight Sir Gawain, who passed by the great
rock under which Merlin had been imprisoned by Nimue. Gawain carried home to
Arthur the last words of the old seer:
Never shall no man speak with me after you,
Therefore it is for nothing that any man should try to seek me out.
Merlin's prophecies continue to intrigue today. Among the events he is said to have foretold are the
erection of the Thames Barrier and the poisoning of the healing waters in the Roman city of Bath, which
have recently been suggested to contain an organism that can cause meningitis.
The magical traditions of the Arthurian legends, as well as those of Merlin, live on in contemporary
literature and cinema. Countless novels appear every year, depicting Merlin in a variety of guises and
setting him in the distant past of Atlantis or the future
world of science fiction. Films, such as John
Boorman's powerfully mythical *Excalibur*,
and the magical television drama *Merlin*
demonstrate that, far from departing,
Merlin continues to return in our own
time, presiding over the ancient realm of
Britain. He remains an enduring and
fascinating presence to this day.

Merlin (Nicol Williamson) reveals
the magical secrets of the dragon
of Britain to Morgan le Fay in the
cavern underneath Camelot in John
Boorman's Excalibur.

Sam Neil as Merlin and Isabella
Rossellini as Nimue in the television
dramatisation Merlin *(National Broad-*
casting Company, 1999), which draws
upon both Dark Age and Medieval
sources for its depiction of the seer's
earthly and other-worldly career.

The Didot Percival relates
how Merlin entered his
'esplumoir' or 'moulting
cage'. While Merlin was so
imprisoned, Sir Gawain heard
his cry and was able to convey
news of the seer's fate to
King Arthur.

A solitary tree overhangs a possible
site for the grave of Merlin. This site,
at Drumelzier in Scotland, is one of
several localities which associate the
area with Merlin.

Back cover: *When times and seasons seem at their end-point, the power
of Merlin returns to help renew and re-envisage the future. Merlin's eter-
nal legacy to the land of Britain is the search for wonder and spiritual
refreshment. (Merlin by Peter Szumowski.)*

Further Reading

Geoffrey of Monmouth *Historiae Regum Britanniae (The History of the Kings of
Britain)* Translated by L. Thorpe. Penguin Books 1965

Geoffrey of Monmouth *Vita Merlini (Life of Merlin)* Edited by Basil Clarke,
University of Wales Press 1973

Makale, Jean Merlin *Priest of Nature* Inner Traditions 1995

Malory, Sir Thomas *Le Morte d'Arthur* Edited by John Matthews, Cassell 2000

Matthews, Caitlín & John *Ladies of the Lake* Aquarian Press 1992

Rich, Deike & Ean Begg *On the Trail of Merlin* Thorson 1991

Stewart, R.J. *The Way of Merlin* Thorson 1991

Tolstoy, Nikolai *The Quest for Merlin* Hamish Hamilton 1985

Stewart, R.J. & John Matthews *Merlin Through the Ages* Blandford Press 1995

Acknowledgements

Photographs and other illustrations are reproduced by kind permission of the following:
Bibliothèque National, Paris: pp.4 (bottom R), 6 (top L); Bodleian Library: pp.5 (top R), 9, 16 (bottom L),
IBC (top); Bridgeman Art Library/British Library: p.4 (bottom L); Bridgeman Art Library/Private collection:
BC, p.16 (top L background); British Library pp.3 (top L), 8 (top R), 10; British Museum: p.6 (bottom R);
Fortean Picture Library: FC; Fortean Picture Library/Paul Broadhurst: p.14 (bottom R); Fotomas Index: pp.2,
3 (background), 11 (centre R); Lambeth Palace Library: p.5 (bottom); Alan Lee (photographed by Pitkin
Unichrome/Mark Slade): p.7; Maas Gallery: p.17 (top L); Mary Evans Picture Library: pp.1, 1 (background),
16 (top L), 16/17 (background), 18 (main); Michael J. Stead: 12 (bottom L), 12 (top), 13, 14 (centre R),
14 (far L), 19 (bottom), IBC (bottom); National Museum of Denmark: p.19 (top); Orion/Kobal Collection:
pp.11 (centre), 20 (bottom L); Pitkin Unichrome: p.11 (top); Pitkin Unichrome/Heather Hook;
p.14 (bottom L); Pitkin Unichrome/Mark Slade: pp.4/5 (background), 6 (background), 8/9 (background),
10/11 (background), 12/13 (background), 14/15 (background), 20/21 (background); Rex Features: p.3
(bottom R); Richard Hooke: p.18 (top R); Stuart Littlejohn: p.17 (bottom); Sven Arnstein/AP: p.20 (R);
Sword in the Stone: pp.IFC, 8 (L), 17 (top R).

Text by John & Caitlín Matthews.
The authors have asserted their moral rights to be identified as the authors of this work.
Edited by Maggie O'Hanlon.
Designed by John Buckley and Simon Borrough.
Picture research by Diana Phillips.
Map by John Buckley.

Publication in this form © copyright Pitkin Unichrome Ltd 2000.
No part of this publication may be reproduced by any means without the permission of Pitkin Unichrome Ltd
and the copyright holders.

Printed in Great Britain.
ISBN 1 84165 021 8   1/00

FS 32611
Pitkin Unichrome is a publishing, design
and photographic company registered to
ISO 9001 by the British Standards Institution.

PITKIN
· GUIDES ·

This guide is one of an extensive series about
FAMOUS PEOPLE · HISTORIC PLACES
Available by mail order
For free colour brochure and full stock list, contact:
Pitkin Unichrome, Healey House, Dene Road, Andover, Hampshire,
SP10 2AA, UK.
**Sales: 01264 409206 Enquiries: 01264 409200
Fax: 01264 334110**
e-mail: guides@pitkin-unichrome.com   website: www.britguides.com

9 781841 650210